Pictures *of the* Afterlife

JUDE NUTTER

With love and kisses

[signature]

salmonpoetry

Published in 2002 by
Salmon Publishing Ltd,
Cliffs of Moher, Co. Clare, Ireland
www.salmonpoetry.com
email: info@salmonpoetry.com

A catalogue record for this book is available from the British Library.

ISBN 1 903392 26 8

Cover artwork: Louis Schiavonetti 1765-1810 British
                    after William Blake 1757-1827
                    Illustration to Blaire's *Grave*:
                    The Soul Exploring the Recesses of the Grave 1808
                    etching
                    23.2 x 11.8 cm
                    Purchased, 1954
                    National Gallery of Victoria, Melbourne, Australia

Cover design & typesetting: Siobhán Hutson

Life was about what could be done with what was left, with what still happened to be there.
   —Adam Philips, *Darwin's Worms*

Acknowledgments

Grateful acknowledgement is made to the following journals in which some of these poems, or earlier versions of them, first appeared:

Alaska Quarterly Review: "Consummation"
Another Chicago Magazine: "Love Walking Out of the Room"
Chiron Review: "Abortion as Ecstasy"
Coracle: "The Paramedics"
Listowel Writers' Week Winners Anthology: "Taste," "The Swan"
Marlboro Review: "University Hospital, Liverpool"
Nimrod: "Wheatfield. With Crows," "Royal Coachman on a Barbless Hook," "Suicide Notes at the End of Summer," "Atomic Nightmare"
Northwest Review: "Thrush"
Poems and Plays #5: "Requiem"
Stand: "Aunt Alice's Ashes"
Water-Stone: "Damage"

For my parents

Contents

Consummation

In the distance Watch Tor, Yes Tor, Devil's Chair.
That press of sky. A few rooks slipping over.
In the ditch, a sprung reed flashing. Your car on its roof
just yards from the river beneath the still oaks,
and the firemen working in their shirt sleeves
to release you. You call me from the hospital,
your voice clearer than I remember, to tell me
you'd understood something sexual in that great solitude,
in the subdued efficiency of voices and the steam
from bodies and the mist off the river gathering together,
a thorough glow inside the water turning under
and under; understood how the blush of sound I make
when I come, my mouth open around the moist, sudden
alarm of the body, is like the voltage of that moment
when light knifes into water just so. When they eased
you out, how you missed, instantly, the poise
of entrapment, your body on the stretcher uncrimping
and suddenly unfaithful in ways you'd never imagined.

That night something inside you turns deftly, like a blade,
edgewise to the light, and I arrive to find your body
slipping gracefully through after it, the dull susurrus
of machinery assuming what you'd always done honestly
for yourself. Then, knowing how sex tormented you
with happiness and to convince you the body knows,
even at the end, what it's good for, I lie down
beside you under the sheets and touch you to hardness.
All night I sleep through your settled, precise silence
and wake early, in darkness, to the oblique, high
clamour of a siren, then crows chattering
their blue light through the world. You will not survive.

You will become a darkness which holds but keeps on
opening. And I will appall all my lovers
by believing wholly in those for whom the world falls

away and is not bribed back. In my hands that cup of bone,
that lost house, the curve of your head for the last time;
and, as if they knew, the nurses coming in to wash you.

University Hospital, Liverpool

1

In the building
where she is dying there are birds
in cages that are still, so convincingly,
birds, on fire
with dark flumes of music. It matters:
the last things the dying hear.

We prayed all day
to a god in whom we could not believe;
not knowing how. All day

those birds
singing, and not tentatively;
their feathers, small coinage
of the body, tipped
from the sills of their cages, drifting
to the floor. The wild irises

by her bed riding
their remote and solemn brightness

2

and whatever gods there are
must love us fiercely
because here is a flower
that has excelled, so shamelessly,
and turned toward the world
with its sex exposed; each blowzy
stamen tongued with colour laid tight
to the petal. And like sex

3

they rescue only the moment.
Never mind
that being loved fiercely
guarantees her nothing. The irises

4

give up their viscid after-scurf of sex.
Such authority of decay. So much
like the smell of bodies after love.

5

All day
we watched her fall
away from prayer: outside

rain coming in
across the Mersey from Wales falling
on the small, sealed leaves of the evergreens,
and the birds, fuming into song and
answering, as they do.

Royal Coachman on a Barbless Hook

In her room at the prow of the house
Where light breaks, and the windows are tossed with linden,
My daughter is writing a story.
    Richard Wilbur

Summer evenings at the kitchen table,
on my grandfather's heavy Remington Portable,
its round keys glowing like bone buttons, I wrote:
sky, with the light in its arms, and *the dusk's*
white dew because sooner or later most of us
sit down and gamble everything

on words. I pounded so hard I threw the type bars
out of alignment, so that certain letters,
scissoring by each other, touched briefly like hands;
and while I put the weight of my whole body
behind what I believed, my father went fishing
on the river Wharfe. *Bird fixed*

like a flame, I wrote, as he stashed
his hip boots, his rod case and creel, his bewitching
selection of flies: *a coffin of shine for the heart.*
And on returning he was always silent: a man
who'd asked for too much and still
come away amazed. So I went to the river—
where the herons stood all day
in the shallows like thin sashays of light and sheets
of water swooned over the weir—and waited
waist high in a chill that held steady, deep

in the current, while my father, with wind-cheating
tight bows, with roll casts, left and right, licked
a Royal Coachman on a barbless hook over the eddies
and riffles. And a marvellous treasure approached us

through darkness. And it would have been simple,
even easy, to drag that fish into the brightness.

But to get that close, to hold a fish like that
and watch the small doors of its gill plates closing
and opening, is to conjure the world
right into your arms and discover how willing,
how ready, how desperate you are to let it go. *So,*
this is how we take the world back, I thought,
piece by piece, and slipped
the hook free, and that fish, with a faint
wash of its tail—a touch so brief
it was unbearable, so final
it was a blessing—poured the chrome light of its body
through the pale fretwork of my fingers and vanished
into the dark tunnel of the river

in which I was standing: in deep, waist deep, arms in it
up to the elbows. Father, I still wake at night
with my hands on fire believing I have a poem
that turns away from death: not, as we are taught
to imagine, by raising the world upward, into the light,
but by releasing it, back
into the pull of the stubborn current.

The 14 Movements: A Prayer for Robert Lee

Those beautiful days
when the city resembles a die, a fan, a birdsong....
        Jaroslav Seifert

1. Parting the Clouds

All my life I've wanted to name the body
in terms of something else, so I drove happily
around the lake to the county morgue thinking *this*
is it, this is it: this is when something violent
and unexpected occurs, just like that, and I walk
away with a great internal sigh of relief
because the soul will not after all turn out
to be something we invent, having nothing else
to put in its place to make the body livable.

2. Waving Hands by the Lake

It was summer, so I stopped by the lake and
with perfect timing a scrub jay arrived; perfect,
because I was trying to name all the possible shapes
for *spirit* and this was an easy one, the size
of a fist. Never had I noticed—been close enough
ever to notice—that eyebrow like a white ellipse,
that vulnerable blush inside the beak, partly open
around the quick salvo of its need: this city
is nothing like birdsong, nothing like a bird,
even though what happens here sometimes is.

3. Chest Expanding on the Mountain

As if dying weren't the worst of it, there we were
in our baby-blue scrubs. There he lay, his thin chest
damp and generous, and I thought

of how a field will stand up against us
in a certain light at evening as the rooks spit over
in handfuls, quietly, and in disarray.
And in that silence before the first cut
I expected the body to be private and expansive
at the same time; as it is

right before you kiss someone you have desired
for a long time, when you foresee,
and are ready for, the instant that changes everything
forever. But the delight is in the quickness of it;

4.   *Painting the Rainbow*

how the ribs and sternum lift off like a shield to reveal
a tight sheen across the arc of the diaphragm and prove
how easy it is to understand one thing in terms of another—
the way light travelling a curve can feel like a bird's
call: a quality of praise we have misunderstood.

5.   *Dove Spreads its Wings*

I understand now
why my mother would sometimes wake me
before dawn and say: *everyone should spend at least
one morning of their life outdoors listening
to the bird chorus greeting the day.*

6.   *Gazing at the Moon*

Why are the least things we can do for each other
always the most difficult. No one had closed
his eyes. And that was the hardest thing of all
to bear. We like to think the dead are lost
without us, but he had lain there so long
with his eyes locked open, beside a stillborn

wrapped in a hospital towel inside a Ziplock bag.
Unheld and unattended
and safe. Waiting, along with all the others.

7.   *Floating Silk in the Air*

The body had gone beyond even the usefulness of its dying
and had nothing to prove; but there were blood-flecked
bubbles at the corners of his mouth, forming and breaking
and forming again. What prayers could we ever invent
against moments like these.

8.   *Sage Presents a Peach*

She had made an incision above his eyes.
In another life, she might have loved him
enough to sit quietly while his spirit
rearranged itself, getting ready; might have slept
fitfully in a chair, getting up hour after hour,
a purling night bird, to peck him awake
with kisses; to place her lips blindly
against his as if pleading with his body like that
might keep it in this world; but in this life
she folded the face down over itself, wiping it
on the inside with a towel to get a good grip, until
he was blindfolded by his own forehead, just
the lips showing and the chin with its shadow
of stubble. The curious, blank treasure of the skull
presenting itself.

9.   *Rowing the Boat in the Lake*

Look what we become when it's all
taken away: the body an empty boat. Everything
removed, sectioned, weighed; and the weights—

those bright sequences of grief, the daily living
reflected in our bodies regardless of injury or habit—

chalked in yellow on a small board while the lab techs,
side by side in blue scrubs, nodded like birds
at the pathologist lecturing on *haemolysis* and *thrombi*
above the quiet hole of his chest: everything going on

toward something measurable. How do we measure
when life leaves the body? We are told: *there is no*
authority above fact and logic, but surely mystery
is the only authority there is. I remember, literally
and without cliché, having his heart in my hands.
It was cut so it fell open, chamber
after chamber, like a book with thick pages.

10. *Scooping Water from the Sea and Viewing the Sky*

I knew already about the small dovetail that's made
when opening the skull; it prevents the skull-
cap from moving when it's replaced.
But I learned that bone, like wood, will bind;
that you have to lean slightly
into the saw; and I found out all about
that quick, wet crack as the cap springs away.

11. *Wind Rustling in the Lotus Leaves*

She was sectioning the brain and I confessed
to how I thought it all looked edible, and she
confessed to wondering if she might be slicing
through a dream, and how fitting this was because dreams
create such practical hungers in us; keep us hungry
for the things we have already. But it's true:
the way she sliced and then spread out
next to him, on a towel with thick, green nap,

appetizers of his own making;
and the colours, those introspective creams and fawns,
a hiatus between the dream and the waking.

12. *Dragon Emerging from the Sea*

There are moments like this,
when the dead hand us every intimacy
the living won't allow: from a stool I could reach
in without leaning to touch the thick ridge
of the spine and search everywhere
for god. And I noticed how she pulled
out his testes and laid each one
gently, across his thigh, on its little string;
that washing him later, she slipped
them back tenderly inside his body.
Tending the dead is the work we are made for.

13. *Windmill Turning in the Wind*

That man could have been my father. But that's
unthinkable.

14. *Breathing in Nature's Fragrance.*

And in the end there's nothing
but the history of the heart's miscalculation:
the hard-won beauty of all that is broken.
In the end, every shred of muscle,
every fragment of bone, was thrown
in a red hazard bag and placed inside the chest
and then the ribs were laid down, the skull-
cap replaced and his face rolled back and the soul

is just the body's cargo, a brief
difficulty we carry everywhere.

Bodies

The foxgloves begin that flickering
descent away from themselves, out

of the visible world: all summer
the narrow sheaths of their flowers

unfurl and the bees, drawn always
by the suck of quiet blooming, arrive

at each slow secret as it rides there
on the thin flame of its stem. And every

flower is bruised hollow with light
and for a while they ignite like the naves

of churches. No wonder the bees
keep nudging beyond the smooth clutch

of the petals and into the widening emptiness
inside those flowers, on fire
with the only burning that counts.

The Swan

And despite myself, I am smiling. Which is to say:
your naked body is beautiful and complete. Which is
what we long for. You are telling me stories
about a patient with a withered arm who follows you
down the hall doing pirouettes, his good arm wavering
over his head, his eyes rolled up toward the ceiling.
He has wing-like material
for an arm you say, moving in tight, flamboyant
circles around the small room. It is late afternoon.
We have been making love. Which is to say we entered
our bodies for a while, and the latent
generosity which then sifts around the heart allows us
to be courageous, in private, about the world's sadness.

I am imagining his wild pirouettes as he follows you
slowly down the hall, knowing, without your saying it,
how you turn toward him and wait; which is to say
I am thinking about a swan I found once, shot down
and abandoned in the marsh for every common

and remarkable reason we don't understand, the large
body tipped over toward its shattered wing. But,
keeping that long neck arched and with its closed beak
barely resting against the earth, it went on testing
its good wing against the air, rowing the body carefully
through wide, uneven orbits in the grass. I had read
how swans mate for life, so I backed away and waited
for the creaking of a single wing to bring down the sky
in the form of a bird like itself. But nothing happened
except the twilight, moving up out of the ground
like it does, until the sky is the last thing

that's possible. I had come to consider the soul
an invention; I questioned its daily arguments
against these bodies we borrow from the earth.
Which is to say, I crawled back through the grass,
humming softly, telling myself I'd kneel there and wait
for as long as it took. It took a long time,
and when it happened I wasn't ready inside
for the pale silence that came after. Which is to say
I had entered the moment that imprisons a heart forever.

ars moriendi

Over the hills the snow
has been falling for a long time.

And your body,
full of small
falling journeys
from which I cannot save you,
has begun its slender
and unholy unfolding.

Outside your room
the sane, ordinary chatter of starlings
is like that brief
volley of rain across the window after dark:
a small, comfortable sound
into which we wake, which stands against
all that wide remoteness we discover
in things that have been falling

for a long time. And yet you are so full
with the bird-like, invisible wisdom
of light and distance, and I am trying

so hard to think of less terrible
or beautiful things.

The Blue Balloon
for Melissa, 1982-1997

Last week it was Easter, but Melissa A. Heinz,
her headstone flush with the earth, was held
secure by a border of eggs marbled purple
and gold, by a wicker basket set down
where her heart should have been.
Inside its woven basin, curios and trinkets:
wrapped chocolates, jewellery, a pinwheel of silver
and green catching the wind
so she might hear it. The world translating itself
into presence. And at her feet, weighed down
by rocks, God, on a postcard. We know
it's God because his face is an absence, an orbit
of emptiness among the bright robes
of his angels. Every one of them
tainted with belief. And the unattainable world
all around in its mosaic of blue. But across
that blue is a message: *Melissa*, it says, *thanks
for all the joy!* And there's a blue balloon,

and lilacs trapped into leaf. I imagine
they arrived as if arriving for dinner: a woman
and a man, struck by the clarity of the world
without her in it, weaving through the brightness
with their bag of gifts and a blue balloon;
that they sank to their knees, like two people
with something important to discuss who kneel
down together in a garden and enter
the shared work love allows. We bring the dead
words. We bring them motion
and colour. And these are the same.
Today I read Rilke to Melissa A. Heinz.
I piss in the grass when I have to. I tell her

about hungers made eternal by absence;
about the box cars of cattle leaving the city
for slaughterhouses out in Austin. I can't tell her
what it means to stand upright over her grave

in spring. In the distance, there's the sound
of one man whistling; then the belch of his backhoe
firing up to fill in someone's grave. No longer
the shovel; no longer the getting down
in one's working clothes to shoulder the slow
accumulation of someone else's grief.
He will roll up the long bolts of fake grass; fold
and stash the heavy tarp he has shaken out
like a sheet across the soil
that came out of the ground. How much,

I ask the dead, does the dirt displaced
by a body weigh. Shouldn't we devour it,
small fistfuls with every meal, for years,
if we need to. The leaves are full with new,
unlikely light and that single balloon
is like a piece of sky come down. The only
hint of eternity I can bear. The gravedigger
begins hauling the moist, dark soil; and the ants,
in their shining bodies, keep labouring up
the long shafts of the grasses until the tiny
weight of their bravery dips them back again
to the earth. Which is more difficult: to believe

in the soul, or admit you have a body. This
is the only question there is; it will enter
your life any way it can
and when you ask it the dead will hand you
the remains of their deepest work.

The Soul Exploring the Recesses of the Grave

etching by Louis Schiavonetti, after William Blake

And so the soul, with a single candle, slips
timidly in where it does not belong, dressed

in a thin shift, without shoes. And why
should it not be curious about the fate

belonging to the body alone. We are not told
that the soul is timid: we are taught that it rises

at the slightest chance,
letting its pedestrian companion go, happily

and with purpose. But how could it not be timid,
faced with its own existence forever.

I think the soul would gladly relinquish
the burden of its immortality

and sit down, here in the one home the body
can afford, pull that thin shift over its knees and wait

in the light of that single candle, diminutive lamp
of the mortal world. We are not told

that the soul is faithful, but why else
would it be found here, trespassing in the ruins.

Aunt Alice's Ashes

emptied on a slough on Sergief Island, Stikine River flats, Alaska

To die here is to vanish
in sudden fire: what begins

with a thin call, like a rush
of water poured from one palm
to another, becomes the marsh hawk

arriving out of nothing. Like a pulse of light.

And it might be longing, or a blunt
sadness nudging the heart,
as the marsh hawk floats out of the open
and back to the trees and shadow.

About me, all evening, all the small
ponds begin to darken, deepen
like bodies opening in ecstasy; like mouths
filling with prayer. The snow geese
blossom up now and then
and on the shimmering distance hang

their impossible whiteness. I believe
a body transformed by fire is somehow

still a body; that you can place it down
inside these gleaming reeds and expect it
to slip quietly away, finally

entering the world as we only hope
to enter death: carried gently
across that remarkable water.

Raising the Dead with Words

They were rabbits mostly, gathered up from mud
and road grit where they'd come to rest, bodies kissed open,
their fur licked flat by the concussion of passing traffic.
And sometimes there was a cat with its bright
grimace of teeth. The world of the dead, erotic
with detail. You thought the gods

entered our lives like this and touching them
realigned your happiness: you could smell it
over the leaf mould and whip of decay.
It was how rain smelled. Singular. And full of privilege.

You arranged your collections across the cellar floor
in boxes: flotillas of boats, with their cargoes prepared,
and your parents grew accustomed to an unshared
sadness, to bodies arranged neatly in rows, to saucers
of milk and torn bread carried on trays down the cellar steps;
even to how you turned from them, doing honestly
the only work you knew, thinking words a sure

blessing. But you were wrong. Or the light
was wrong, or the world
missed the perfect confluence of your heart
and its intention because those bodies kept moving
with invisible inertia to wherever it is
bodies move to. Once there was a starling

shoved from its nest, featherless and grotesque,
peppered with clippings of mown grass,
and only just alive. Yet your father remembers
otherwise: that it was dead before
you found it, fused shut around air and brilliance,
like a word fallen into the world. What good

is belief if it isn't useful: *starling*, you whispered,
lips pressed to its translucent skin,
because the body was benevolent and on your side;
because it sounded like *darling*, a likely name for holiness.

Love Walking out of the Room

for *Denise du Maurier and Zetta Huot*

The rain falls with less beauty,
now, to the open ground, and the shadows of crows
pass freely over the lawn. Here is an absence
that will never be undone by even the busy work
of wings. Your mother is dying. And a storm
has thrown down the cottonwood outside your window.

Pavlova's dying words, your mother says, were a quiet request
that her swan costume be made ready; and Elizabeth Browning
in reply to Robert, who had asked how she felt, said
beautiful.   And such a thing it is that carries
us over: the slight vessel words can make. This,

your mother tells you, is the final trick pulled from the dark
sleeve of the body; a wisdom we spend our lives
perfecting. It's what goes with us, beyond reach.

There are no swans here. But each evening, as you wheel
her along that footpath between the river
and the open fields, there are Carolina grasshoppers
carrying their durable bodies between dark wings
hemmed with yellow. Like the right words, they arrive
when you stop looking, and your mother is happy
with their singing; with the way they launch themselves
out from under her wheels and vanish
into the grass. When she tires

of this you know there is nothing
more to be done. There are no heroics: *hospice, please*,
she says; *ashes, please*, and then stops asking
for what she wants. But you tell her anyway
how your heart invented the permanence

of the world for its own sake and came to depend
completely on the private erasure
of leaves, on a formal solitude it could enter
without going anywhere. You spend a whole morning

bullying one, small grasshopper into a jar,
which you then slip inside your purse and smuggle
past the nurses. Beside her bed it tests the boundaries
of its surprising world, its body tapping
patiently against the thin glass for hours until
you release it at last into the room where it sings
from the lax folds of the flowered curtains, from the silver
sling of the U-bend beneath the sink; sings, even,
from the pockets of the jacket your mother
has chosen and hooked over a print of van Gogh's
Bedroom in Arles, shrouding

all its gold. After it alights there's always a final
blink of yellow as a Carolina grasshopper folds
away the cloak of its wings, and it's like that moment
when you look up just in time to catch
the last glimpse of someone you love walking

out of a room: an iridescent button, perhaps,
against the cuff of a blouse, or the polished heel of a shoe;
the shoulder of a favourite jacket frisked with rain.
And your mother is listening
because the consequences of not listening
are always dire. *How lucky we are*, she says,
from the threshold to whatever realm it is
she has been testing, *that some doors stand open
forever.*

Damage

...the melancholy of the purely physical.
John Updike

Every day I walked into the small hospital room and offered
my father nothing. On good days he would bicker with the nurses,

but mostly he lay turned to the window, watching the leaves
create within themselves a silent, aqueous gloom

that had nothing to do with silence. Sometimes he talked
in his sleep, but mostly he just moved his lips in an epilepsy

of quiet, happily reclaiming things forgotten from his life
and I put my mouth down on his to inhale the inaudible

weight of his joy. His skin was almost blue, like sky slammed
open over an ocean in summer; and his soul, floating in its pale

container, had the darkest shine. When my father died
right next to me, I went home to my lover and said nothing;

I unzipped him, took his cock into the cave of my mouth
and when he sank down afterward, leaning

forward, there was a light suspended there inside his shirt, the tiny
desolation of lust caught by surprise outside the body and then

he whispered *you know, sex is not what you think it i*s and I knew

he never would love my loneliness out of me. I still can't bear
the way he stood up and buckled his pants, his hands threading

the soft leather through the buckle of his belt, but I opened
    my thighs
to him anyway, let him touch the small violence of skin above

my stockings as if the body's deep privacies could be ripped
away; I thought about those last seconds when my father was living;

how he turned from the window, as if refusal of this world
were an act of faith; how I'd placed my long bones down
    against his

on the narrow hospital bed, opening my mouth to the dark, vast
presence of his hair as if something might cross over into me

when it mattered most; how I'd lain happily
in my own body. How I'd let that be enough.

The Annunciation

I knew right away the Angel Gabriel
was nothing but trouble: any stranger

wafting through your house on wings and afflicted light
must be ripe with some form of treachery. Besides,

I'd seen it on television—how a woman and a man
stand close together with their clothes still on

breathing into each other's mouths and then,
miraculously, a week later in the next episode,

she's pregnant. So when I found that condom
in the pine copse behind the school gymnasium,

even though I was fully clothed, even though
I only pushed it around a bit with a stick, it felt

inevitable because there was a redpoll jigging
like a flame high above my head

in the evergreens, and the short cries
only boys can make floated up from the playing fields

and gathered, like the silence
of wings, in the undergrowth.

What better way could we ever have invented
to circumnavigate the flesh. It's true: our taste

for eternity begins early, and the angels are seductive
and insistent; their words

smoulder in air like afterimages of tiny rooms in heaven
so that any man seems inadequate, trapped

in a clew of muscle and sweat. Imagine Joseph,
the unstable talus of suspicion inside his heart

forever; or Gabriel, his body
like a durable overcoat, going back to his real life

ruined and incomplete, as would any man
who couldn't make love to a woman

the gods had chosen. Against her will. But I know
why a woman might let this happen and go on

with her work while the inconvenience
of the body—the only

scaffold we can pin our grief on—vanishes in fire.

Abortion as Ecstasy

This is how it happens:

1

I knock back Percodan and Dixie cups of brandy.
I take the luggage of this body toward that bright tray

of final instruments; toward those accoutrements
of the luckless: paper sheets and stirrups; boxes
of swabs and rubber gloves; the bottles of Betadine,

each one labelled *for individual use*. Outside the door,
along the smooth, grey hospital corridor, the crepe-soled
concern of the nurses comes and goes.

2

When it is over, I drive home through the sharp October
afternoon with whatever it is he has taken from me
in a box on the back seat. Over the blank expanse
of the marsh the hawks shear and cross, the light
sometimes granting them an angle of certain fire,

sometimes an armour of chrome. And with a stretched
ecstasy of abandon they rise up from the grasses
so suddenly. And how easily sex makes its grave

3

inside the body. Like this. The hawks rise up
through the brightness, perfect. And possible.

4

And whatever it is he has taken from me
I burn on the beach at low tide, hoping something
might rise through the oiled tightness of the water:
not male, not female; but beyond and better
than that. It's the idea of life I love. How selfish
of the dead to never lie finally down. There is
silence. And water. Both empty.
Both enormous. And such a little ghost.

Alex Corville's *Seven Crows*

Perhaps the birds do inherit
the loveliest part of what we are. Every day

the crows unclose for us
like the lips of the dead:
under occasional sunlight the slick-hard
kiss of each body simply unlocks
as they break from the forest. Perhaps

we travel forever in that thin boat
of ribs, cradled behind the dark, busy

hearts of the birds. And maybe this
is how the dead unfasten
toward belonging, shot through
with irregular fire. Maybe this

is how we all get taken, one
from another. Are you ready to believe
that the soul would ask for this airy cathedral

that is the body of a bird, for a final body
more perfect than any you imagined
which rises off the earth at dawn and at the end
of each day comes back to settle
like a leaf on the roofless world?

Taste

There is no way to say this in any terms other
than its own: how your father once led you
into the open air—a harmless gesture and one
expected from a father toward his son
when he has discovered something precious
to hand over from inside his own heart.
But why expect only kindness from those
we confess to love: now we must imagine an act
too terrible to happen. It happened. Then,
we must imagine your spirit actually breaking.
And then imagine what that means.
There are no details about how you were standing,
if you were hiding your small fists inside
your pockets, or even about what you were wearing:
it was just your father, in sunlight; your father
who has never once believed in the luxury of love,
pulling the rabbit from its cage, his massive arm
raising the club, the tiny skull giving way
and the whole world reduced to this

while your body made those moves it needed
to survive, letting the mind, letting
the heart, that visceral organ of hope, unlatch
from every familiar hook of trust,
from any possibility of god: the quick dismissal
of intuitive happiness. And later: your father
at the head of the table, forcing you to eat his belief
in the foolishness of loving anything
for its own sake, as things must be loved, without
relief, if they are to carry us. And how, after that,
everything in this world tasted bad. You love
with difficulty now. So, come: let's take
that small boy by the hand and walk him back

across the garden to that crude hutch under the trees,
unloose the rabbit from that dark cage and touch,
for the first time, a life we have now chosen
to continue. We will marvel
at how a body can grow less vigilant in the presence
of love. We will trust, as hard and for as long
as we need, that the lope of a rabbit through tall grass
is the only act of grace we require; in the world
as it could be if our hearts were kind.

The Afterlife

So, linking arms like schoolgirls, my mother and I wander
all afternoon from store to store without finding
the one eye shadow she is counting on to complete
her outfit. *Try to remember*, I suggest, *the name
of the shade you want. I don't need to*, she says: *I'll know it*

as soon as I see it. But that night she decides
to name her own hue; so, in her darkened kitchen,
in our dressing gowns and slippers, my mother and I
invent the possibilities together: *Paradisio,
Smokey Rose, The Last Unknown Location
of the Soul*: wild names that made us grateful. When she dies

I will stand over her grave and repeat these words down
into the soil, because these are the words women use
to name their love for each other, in a kitchen
after midnight, while a gale rattles
the roof tiles and the shipping forecast blooms

from the radio so they can't help thinking
about those men out on the vast smear of the Atlantic,
dressed in oil skins and damp wool, playing cards and smoking
below deck, while the first mate stands in the unshared
silence of the pilot house navigating
the dull physicality of this world. Sometimes

there's nothing better for a woman
than the loneliness of one man, the weather itself

the only cause for alarm. But my mother is afraid
she won't recognize my father in the next life. *This
is my biggest fear*, she says. It has replaced whatever dread
it was that kept her moving between my brother's room

and mine as we slept our way across the vast country
of childhood. I think of her wandering forever, tired
of immortality, because what hope is there,

even in a world beyond this one, without love. *How*, I say,
could you fail to know him, thinking she will simply slip
between the burdens of the familiar world into an evening
of light rain, with her collar turned up and her best gloves on,
to find my father trimming the privet
with a pair of well-oiled shears, wearing the jacket
she once patched at the elbows with ovals of dark leather,
the top button of his shirt securely fastened; that he will

come forward, an unnamed shade only she will recognize,
the colour of sea wrack and surf, with the coarse dirt
under his fingernails and the scent
of something feral—badger or fox. And crushed grass.

Atomic Nightmare

How should we dream of this place without us?
Richard Wilbur

Flesh is the one possession we carry:
what other burden would we need. It's the only
sorrow we believe we'll never lay down.

And how much we depend on the world's fidelity!
without it there is no self, and our memories
are only useful if some of us survive. Look,

even the smallest and the most common of things:
the disused train track overhung with honeysuckle;
the rind of an apple peeled off

and flung on the table in a continuous strip
like a green banner; the smell light makes
when it hits water. *How should we dream*

of this place without us? and what happens
in the heart when nothing is safe: not the headlands
frantic with light and the luminous wings of Adonis

blues; not the young pheasants scrambling
out of the green corn, their cries like small rocks
rattling in a bucket; not even the slow shrug

of the river. Herons and swans alive on the dark
water. The boles of the great beeches slick with rain.
I create, said Rauschenberg, *in that gap between art*

and life, and I knew he meant that silence
through what little we can use must pass; that absence
across which one darkness reaches out

toward another: I was sixteen, alive
in a new Europe bristling with missiles,
and I had no language but art. Upstairs, in the spare

room turned into a studio so I could paint, I would slip
free of my clothes, cover my strange, unrequested
body with the darkest pigment I could find and place

myself down against long sheets of paper. Classical
music drifted up through the floorboards as my mother
prepared meals in the kitchen below. And when I chose

to stand, there I was: the small orbs
of my breasts and belly, the long slabs of my own thighs:
the shadow of someone

in an act of passing—a record of my own
disappearance. And that was the summer
I began to starve myself and drink: vanishing

on my own terms. Now, in middle age, the world
again on the rim of war, the old fear quivers
at the lip of the mind, and the man I love admits

the greatest fear he ever had was that he might die
before making love to a woman. He's outlived
his terror, of course, more than once. But mine

is the same: that I'll never come close to finding
the one word for what it feels like to live, even
for a short while, and then survive long enough

to believe it true.
And still, I think it will happen without warning
during summer: my mother will be singing

along with the radio, making salad, and under
her fingers the carrots and leaves
of lettuce will explode into ribbons of light, and then

the sliced cucumber into wheels of flame; and then
she and her singing and my father,
who will be out in the garden, shuttling back

and forth with the mower, will simply flail
into sheets of fire. My father's garden, in which,
because it's summer, all the birds of Ireland

will be singing. Did the songs
sung by the birds of Hiroshima burn into shadows,
too, like bodies? Even a song has a body.

And as for me, my vanishing occurred so early
I'd never be astonished to discover
impressions of myself everywhere, reaching out,

across that darkness.

Wheatfield. With Crows

There are many things I should like to write you about,
but I feel it is useless.
   Vincent van Gogh

Imagine van Gogh returning exhausted after painting
all day in the fields. Since dawn, he has been dipping hopefully
into the difficult solitudes of the heart. He has been doing this
all his life. There is wisdom inherent in pathos: the Egyptians

removed everything except the heart from the strung pavilion
of the body, which then rode forward, with provisions,
toward the contradictions of its afterlife. We send the heart out,
day after ordinary day, willingly and in terror. *I am ravished*,
wrote van Gogh, *ravished with what I see….* Imagine
loving one thing enough you would give your life for it:

that nightingale heard when you were twelve, perhaps;
or the time you walked in on your father stepping naked
from his morning bath, and the way you admonished
and then, later still, forgave yourself for looking, not up
in rapture, but to the body, whose bright haul

downward none of us resist. And so, to the lilac and grasses.

Or that moment someone said *you must be lonely*
for the world to seem so lonely, and you discovered
you were, because the world the heart inherits is its own;
or a sky the colour of pewter, the right body against
your own and outside a salvo of rain against the roof
like a threat of harm: the paradox of loveliness and hurt.
Or how, on winter afternoons, one crow arrives ahead
of the rest to the cottonwood outside your window
and, lifting its whole body with the effort, calls to others
across the city block. They call each other home like this,
tree by tree. *Home*, we say. Meaning the place we lie down

and rest; the place a heart must ultimately go, deeply
and with cause. Think of van Gogh, painting that spatter
of crows furling out over the wheat; dragging
into the safe stillness of art, one untiring wing after another,
a translation of the failed dream we greet every morning
as we set out, tired from being trapped
in a human form without wings. *My ambition*, wrote van Gogh,
*is limited to a few clods of earth, sprouting wheat, an olive grove,
a cypress.* The work of the heart has nowhere else to go.

The Paramedics

What does it mean that one of us drives home
through the early morning, pulls his wife
from the bed where she is sleeping and kisses her
hard on the mouth—hard, to prolong his own silence,
and then without undressing makes love to her
with such ruinous hunger she is almost afraid;
or that one of us doesn't make it home
but stops instead at a bar in an unfamiliar town
that she has driven to on purpose in an attempt
to believe she still has choices, and drinks
until she allows some man to persuade her back
to his bed, display and unbolt her body; or
that one of us, in the back of an ambulance
with a patient she knows won't make it,
reaches out on impulse to touch her partner,
her gloved hand leaving a blood print
across his chest, and that he leans into her, kissing
her back, because they can't get close enough,
often enough, to reinvent the wholeness
of the body; and that after the shift this continues
when they go home together and undress slowly,
and stroke the other's body all day, unashamed
of their own sorrow, as if sorrow might be
a place they could inhabit; or that one of us,
after restocking the ambulance, waits in the rig
with the lights turned off because he likes
the cathedral sadness of it and how a small light
from the outside on the doors of the cabinets
and on the equipment makes, like prayer,
a great distance in him; that sometimes he is a man
emptied of everything but his own need?

Suicide Notes at the End of Summer

Bright mornings.
Days when I want so much I want nothing.
Just this life, and no more.
    Raymond Carver

I don't know what it feels like to want death
more than you want this life: in the mornings,
in the early light, I simply do my work, writing
to salvage whatever it is that might have fallen away
in darkness; glancing up now and then
toward that house across the garden, whose tenants
I barely knew, whose roof shines privately behind
the rain, like the closed eyes of a woman made up
for the grave, or for love. Sparrows and juncos—
black-capped, small birds—move unnoticed almost
inside the fine contusion of the trees and the grass
turns silver under the wind. Its brightness
makes me tired. I salvage the world
in manageable portions. But *salvage* is one,
thin consonant away from *savage*, and which privacy
seems more so: mine, where I give my despair first
one shape, then another, arriving at nothing; or his,
which was unequivocal. What frightens me now is not
that he did it, but how he must have hung, perhaps
spinning a bit, perhaps swinging, all week long
while I did my work, looking up and toward him now
and again to test its propositions; while I drank,
manufacturing the only tenderness
out of which I could make love to a man and then
leave him abandoned, like a word set down on the page.
Or lay alone in darkness, listening for the small sound
of rain in the grasses and to the last fruits
dropping, with their quick chatter, through the leaves
of the apple tree. Even though I might not

know what it means to want death more
than you want this life, I know what a feat it is
to inhabit the dark
chapel of a human heart where there is nothing
beyond the vista of your own introspection.
I heard that when they cut him down his girl
fell on him and pressed her lips, hard, against his.
But how did she move beyond faith and into belief,
like this? And how many of us can say
we would search like that for the unnameable
taste inside the mouth of someone we love;
that we could cherish one thing so clearly, or so well?

His Mother with her Hands among Flowers

for Chris

There was nothing mysterious about it;
it was simply one young boy coming home
through the rain, walking into the solitude
of a house empty since morning, laughing
into the shining gap of relief that happens
right after a storm when it feels as if something
difficult has just been said; then looking out
across the garden to see his dead mother
moving from flowerbed to flowerbed, working.
No wings, no halo, no sheen from the otherworld;
nothing miraculous or grand: just his mother,
in a worn, loose-knit sweater, weeding
and picking up petals spread through the garden
with the rain, her hands lost among flowers, loving,
as she did in this life, any avenue out of despair.

He knew his loss to be ordinary; that the world
would refuse him even the slightest language
for it. So, what possible use could there ever
have been for prayer. It was summer and I know

what courage it took waking each day
and not replacing death with something better.
No one else would have been sad enough
to notice her slight, single hesitation
as a skylark overhead blistered into song;
how she placed each petal down on the same,
low stone of the rockery and then knelt
for a long time in the wet grass, untangling
all the small blossoms smacked flat together
in the downpour. The body asks
for what it needs; for what makes it whole.

I know he stood there, afraid he would ever need
anything more than a garden full of small
exclamations as the leaves of the privet caught
the late afternoon light; a loneliness
through which nothing has fallen all day
except the rain. Because what reward it finally is
to discover the dead have nowhere further to go.

Hermes Delivers Flowers to the Hospice

Because we see the grave
is the size of a door....
        Richard Jones

I come burdened by petals and private flame,
with baby's-breath and lilies, sprigs
of eucalyptus with their scent of attics
and lost memory and
here and there an iris like a soul
in its thimble of fire.
But what of the soul?   It withdraws

from the body in secret.   Even
when you pay attention, leaning close,
its departure is private
and ordinary: one person
leaving another.   With vague, abstract
gratitude I will be remembered,

like a day of exceptional weather.
Because I am the one who stops
at the curb, leaps out against traffic,
gathers the evidence into my arms,
and enters.   And of course the grave

is the size of a door: you imagine
your dead coming and going,
never anything less than bodies.
In the bright corridors I walk immune

to the false politeness of grief, the soles
of my shoes squeaking on the grey linoleum,
where those of you who know what relief it is
to leave behind the specific

miracle of the flesh, the one loneliness
common to you all, sleep through

the tedium of late afternoon.
The essential stranger, I enter
the circle of affection
to safely give away what isn't mine;
and you wake, covered by the caul
of dream, and turn the shining discs
of your faces toward me, making of hope
an obvious thing. Even though at birth

you were lost already, borne into debt.
Maybe the grave is the only

door that leads you anywhere,
but how would you know: your dead open
the way. Then close it quietly
against you forever. Sometimes,
on the threshold of a doorway the size
of a grave, I speak a name

and you do not rise to meet me
out of your dying. I tell you,

after death the body is an entrance
into an absence the colour of ashes
and bone. A silence
even gods won't meddle with.

Self-portrait in the Bathroom Mirror
by Pierre Bonnard

Even though all reference to the memory
of Marthe's body consumed by light
and withdrawing is gone, he has still given in

to the constant bickering of nostalgia: the light
still arrives from outside the picture but now
it feels closer, almost audible—the body's low

nag of loneliness humming
along his left clavicle and through the thin flesh
of his left ear. She has been dead

almost four years. His gaze
is permanently fixed now on that brush
and the half-empty bottles of scent arranged
along the shelf before his mirror: the only objects

not rendered as reflections
of themselves. They must be hers.

Stranded in Paradise—International Departures, Gate 15

Even the Lord, you are thinking, knew generosity
worked metaphorically, disguising our estrangement
as something better: *take this*, he said, *and eat—*
for this is my body. And here you all are, dividing

yesterday's paper between you and slyly cracking open,
against regulations, your litres of duty-free liquor; bound
for, or travelling away from, the one landscape
you call home. Then out come the snapshots

of children and lovers and other, small guarantees
against exile, but you have just buried your father
and so the only history you can offer is the smell
of damaged grass around the doorway to his grave.

Here's my husband, says the woman beside you,
at home in Manitoba—and there he is, his shirt
unbuttoned and a whip-crack of light along the seam
of horizon behind him. You have no pictures, but deep

in your pockets there are nests of crushed grass torn
from the fringes of your father's grave, and the smell
of crushed grass, you tell her, is the only home
you will agree to because all we can recall of paradise

is the tang of the ruined acres beneath our bodies
as we rolled over. *Home*, she sighs,
really is where the heart is, isn't it? And you think,
yes; but only if the heart sets up camp in the place

where its dead are buried and doesn't mind leaving
its boots outside all night in the rain or sleeping
in a bag with a broken zipper. The heart must dig
deeply in and outlast its own bewilderment

and its terror—there are going to be times,
even in daylight, when the small creatures of the hills
and hedgerows break into camp and scatter
all the heart's meagre provisions wildly about the fields.

Requiem

1

The grey herons drift
into the shallows like rafts

of joy. When they move
I believe it to be

simply the mind moving them for us,
because the mind can discover

no reference for stillness
such as theirs.

2

We received news
of your death and found ourselves

no longer afraid.
We had become fearful of you

falling away from us daily
by degrees: it was every

betrayal of your body we feared
never this marvellous

stillness at the end of it.

3

So. It's that delicate
grief I want, the uncommon

comfort of a brief, particular loneliness
on an evening in summer

when the trees become private
with light

so every bloom on the mountain ash
is a closed door of brightness

and there's that incandescent
and astonishing relief

because their final push
out of themselves
is over at last.
The crows weave home
wearing the last

flicker-black gloaming, the colour
of light, working:

there's that glisten-deep
racket of their returning and

in that quick, oiled
rattle of feathers, an echo

like a rearranging
of garments, like the solidity
of longing and this
is grief and this

4

is how it happens.

Thrush

A thrush has unlocked the sudden, slim
tunnel of its throat. And like a blind
fall toward a promise of joy, here comes

that final song. All evening
the hawkmoths have scissored
and displayed and crossed

the threshold of each brilliant flower.
Such gestures, of course so like our own,
are of the body's making, are the deep

weights that need can become.
And we enter the liquid ache
of the thrush's terminal song, that place

where something stunning keeps on
beginning, and there,
the long brightness we might truly be

lets go. And with the blowzy
splay of the physical, we open forward.

The Butterfly Collector
Camping in Spain, 1972

At night, when even my nakedness didn't feel
like my own, when all it proved
was that clothes frame unanswerable questions
about the body, I'd watch the silhouettes
of the French couple in the tent pitched
next to ours: sometimes, I saw them undress; heard
admissions wring loose from inside them. Later

I'd understand how when we rummage
through each other during love, it's the animal
inside our bodies we're after, not the spirit.

Not once did they fail at being beautiful; they laughed
the next day in greeting, buoyed up by the aftermath
of what they thought had gone on in secret.
Then one day, after the police had found her,
that woman came weeping and gesturing
for my father to please drive her
straight to the hospital and then perhaps take her
to collect whatever she could salvage
from their car, which had been towed to a lot
on the edge of another town. All afternoon
I roamed with my killing jar and nets, hooking
emperors and swallowtails off the wild herbs.
They died fading into something better.
As if angels of undiminished tenderness and care
inside their small bodies roved back and forth, back

and forth. I imagined the doctors telling her:
we almost lost him, as if they had simply
set him carelessly aside; not because
he'd been roaming for a time, undecided.

She and my father returned with a back seat full
of maps and possessions, and what I remember
most about my first lessons in intimacy
and terror is one fawn-coloured cushion branded
with a wild cascade of blood, which my father
handed to me as I stood there lost
in my twelve-year-old body for the last time,
under the evergreens and the bleak
Mediterranean light, letting the angels go.

Directions to the Lady Lever, Port Sunlight

Take the 8:15 from Lime Street because it runs
along the estuary; because it's the non-commuter,
the milk run, and from every window
you'll watch brightness drop in great panels
over the water. You might think these are doorways
sprung open in the world

and left unguarded, but this is something
only the dead know, and the dead
tell us almost nothing about where they belong.

In the museum, as the guards in their solemn uniforms
and serious shoes float through the quiet galleries,
sidle from canvas to canvas: here
is Burne-Jones' Merlin, languishing on a branch
and suffering his beguilement, the tips of his fingers
lost in frilled darkness among the blossoms

of a hawthorn; and there, in a still life, tight
clusters of grapes, the panes of a window reflected,
in miniature, in almost every fruit; and it's clear
that to tease a flower open toward presence
you simply fix blisters of dew among its petals.

Here is a world where even a fat hare
draped over the edge of a table is granted an easy
stretch along the whole length of its body and,
behind the grimace of its dead lips, something slight
and demure, as if the spirit were an animal misplaced
inside the idea of the flesh. See how we invent

the idea of beauty and place it
beyond the limits of our own dying; how it becomes
our secular prayer. All day,
whatever it means to be human will remain

hidden but always present
as an act of will: the stubborn heart bullied from secrecy.

Ten minutes before closing, in a room
of Chinese ceramics, discover something useful: *a small,*
rectangular box, the guidebook will tell you, *inside of which*
is a model of a two-storied dwelling, with staircase;
inhabitants missing. Their absence will feel honest:
there's a basket of fruit at the foot of the stairs
and two pairs of slippers, side by side, on a table
next to the bed, which is much too narrow
for more than one body. These extra slippers

are for the dead we greet in dreams, or for those
who come solely for the comfort of love
and do not stay, and surely these are one and the same
because it makes no difference to the imagination
if the beds on which we lie down to love
are narrow.

Walk home, then, along the wastes of the estuary
where the lights on the refinery towers wink
off and on and the slick mud of the flats
glistens like a flung sheet of sky. People die here:
bait hunters in waders; boys from the council estates
in their secondhand clothing assuming

they've nothing to lose; and young couples
stranded in row boats who vault over the gunwales,
their instincts elsewhere—lovers
locked up to their waists in mud, wavering
in the crosscurrents like pallid reeds, with their hands
raised toward the water's metallic underbelly
and their eyes squeezed shut. As if
there might be one, final salvation still possible
to imagine. *Art is generous,*

you once heard yourself proclaim
at a party and only now, as you travel toward home
through fresh darkness and rain, will you know
what that means. Art is the only labour

that succeeds by omission: between what we imagine
and what's finally rendered is a world
where only beautiful things that cannot exist are discovered;
where the dead fall back into their clothes and slippers.